GODOT IS A WOMAN

RENARD PRESS — PLAYSCRIPT V

GODOT IS A WOMAN

SILENT FACES THEATRE

RENARD PRESS

RENARD PRESS LTD

124 City Road
London EC1V 2NX
United Kingdom
info@renardpress.com
020 8050 2928

www.renardpress.com

Godot is a Woman first published in 2022

Text © Silent Faces Theatre Ltd, 2022
Cover by Will Dady, based on a design by Josie Underwood
Cover portraits © Ali Wright, 2022

Printed in the United Kingdom by Severn

ISBN: 978-1-80447-014-5

9 8 7 6 5 4 3 2

Silent Faces Theatre assert their right to be identified as the author of this work in accordance with the Copyright, Designs and Patents Act 1988.

This is a work of fiction. Any resemblance to actual persons, living or dead, is purely coincidental.

All rights reserved. This publication may not be reproduced, stored in a retrieval system or transmitted, in any form or by any means – electronic, mechanical, photocopying, recording or otherwise – without the prior permission of the publisher.

Permission for producing this play may be applied for via the publisher, using the contact details above, or by emailing rights@renardpress.com.

CONTENTS

Godot is a Woman   9

Acknowledgements   65
About Silent Faces   67

GODOT IS A WOMAN

*To the women, non-binary and trans people
throughout history who fought for our right to exist
unapologetically and for our voices to be heard.
And to the queen of pop herself, Madonna.*

Notes on casting and performance

In performance, the performers' names (Josie, Jack and Cordelia) should be substituted with the names of the performers playing those roles. For casting, we suggest Cordelia and Josie be played by female performers and Jack be played by a trans masc non-binary performer.

A tree-like structure stands to one side of the stage and a roadside telephone box to the other. Hold music plays from the telephone and breaks intermittently with recorded messages.

PHONE VOICEOVER: Thank you for calling the Beckett Estate. Your call is important to us. Please continue to wait and an operator will be with you shortly.

(*There are three people in the space:* JOSIE, JACK *and* CORDELIA. JACK *has no trousers on. In fact, all three of them are half-dressed. They crowd around the roadside telephone. During the following action they finish getting dressed: raggedy suits, boots and bowler hats like those worn by the characters in* Waiting for Godot. *They wait until the hold music cuts out.*)

PHONE VOICEOVER: Thank you for calling; your call is number – eight – in the call queue. Please continue to wait and an operator will be with you shortly.

(*The hold music continues and they wait until the music cuts out.*)

PHONE VOICEOVER: Your call is number – seven – in the call queue.

(*The hold music continues. They wait.* CORDELIA *begins to subtly dance to the music, bending at the knees. The other two join in and the three of them gradually dance across the stage and back again in rhythm with the music. The hold music cuts out.*)

PHONE VOICEOVER: Thank you for calling; your call is important to us.

(*The hold music continues and they wait until the music cuts out.*)

PHONE VOICEOVER: Your call is number – four – in the call queue.

(*The hold music continues. The monotony of the hold music puts* JACK *into a trance-like state. The other two join them, looking into the middle-distance. They are all briefly entranced until the music cuts out.*)

PHONE VOICEOVER: Your call is number – four – in the call queue.

A tree-like structure stands to one side of the stage and a roadside telephone box to the other. Hold music plays from the telephone and breaks intermittently with recorded messages.

PHONE VOICEOVER: Thank you for calling the Beckett Estate. Your call is important to us. Please continue to wait and an operator will be with you shortly.

(*There are three people in the space:* JOSIE, JACK *and* CORDELIA. JACK *has no trousers on. In fact, all three of them are half-dressed. They crowd around the roadside telephone. During the following action they finish getting dressed: raggedy suits, boots and bowler hats like those worn by the characters in* Waiting for Godot. *They wait until the hold music cuts out.*)

PHONE VOICEOVER: Thank you for calling; your call is number – eight – in the call queue. Please continue to wait and an operator will be with you shortly.

(*The hold music continues and they wait until the music cuts out.*)

PHONE VOICEOVER: Your call is number – seven – in the call queue.

(*The hold music continues. They wait.* CORDELIA *begins to subtly dance to the music, bending at the knees. The other two join in and the three of them gradually dance across the stage and back again in rhythm with the music. The hold music cuts out.*)

PHONE VOICEOVER: Thank you for calling; your call is important to us.

(*The hold music continues and they wait until the music cuts out.*)

PHONE VOICEOVER: Your call is number – four – in the call queue.

(*The hold music continues. The monotony of the hold music puts* JACK *into a trance-like state. The other two join them, looking into the middle-distance. They are all briefly entranced until the music cuts out.*)

PHONE VOICEOVER: Your call is number – four – in the call queue.

(*The hold music continues.* JOSIE *finds the speakerphone button. The hold music blares from the speaker.* JOSIE *hangs up the phone and the music continues. They are impressed. They all walk away from the phone, seeing how far they can go. The music cuts out and they all run back to the phone.*)

PHONE VOICEOVER: For more information on obtaining performance rights to Beckett's works please see our website at www.beckettfoundation.org.uk/rights.

(*The hold music continues and they wait until the music cuts out.*)

PHONE VOICEOVER: Your call is number – three – in the call queue.

(*The hold music continues. They are starting to get nervously excited now. The music cuts out.*)

PHONE VOICEOVER: Your call is number – two – in the call queue.

(*The hold music continues. They prepare themselves for the phone to finally be answered until…*)

PHONE VOICEOVER: Thank you for calling the Beckett Estate. There is no one available to answer your call at the moment, so please leave a message at the tone and someone will get back to you. (*Beep noise.*)

(*Throughout the following* JOSIE *gets increasingly faster, rambling and flustered.*)

JOSIE: Oh… Um… HI! Hi! Hello, this is Josie calling from Silent Faces… We're a theatre company… We've been in touch a few times about the performance rights for *Waiting for Godot*, mainly via email, but we've tried calling a couple of times, and I've also written a letter… or two or… anyway, we're really pushed for time now, so we were just calling to see if we could maybe talk to someone about moving forward with our application as soon as possible, so if someone could get back to us that would be great. I think you have my number in the emails I have sent you, so yeah, if someone could just get in touch that would be great. OK, thanks, love you, bye. (*Puts the phone down.*)

(JACK *and* CORDELIA *look at* JOSIE *in embarrassment.*)

JACK: What was that?

(*Pause.* JOSIE *squirms.*)

JACK: It's awful.

(*The hold music suddenly blares.*)

PHONE VOICEOVER: You are number – 8,524 – in the call queue.
CORDELIA: Can I have a hug?
JACK: Yeah, of course.

(*They hug.*)

JACK: What do we do now?
JOSIE: We wait.
JACK: Yes, but while we wait?
CORDELIA: We could play at being them.
JOSIE: Vladimir and Estragon?
CORDELIA: No.
JOSIE: Being who?
JACK: The ones in the know.
JOSIE: They could explain.
CORDELIA: They would—
JACK: Clarify.
JOSIE: The universal truth givers.

(*Pause.*)

RADIO VOICEOVER: This is BBC Radio 4.

(*Four radio pips play.*)

CORDELIA: You first.
JACK: After you.
JOSIE: I insist.

(*A radio voiceover plays. They lip-sync to the it, impersonating each character.*)

ALL (*lip-syncing*): 'Nothing happens… It's awful.'
JOSIE (*lip-syncing*): So speaks one of the characters in a play by the then little-known Irish writer that ended up changing theatre for good.
CORDELIA (*lip-syncing*): And, indeed, when Samuel Beckett's *Waiting for Godot* hit the stage for the first time in 1955, the early reviews were rather similar to that line from the play…
JOSIE (*lip-syncing*): It really felt like history was being unfurled right before my eyes. I could feel the time passing… slowly.
CORDELIA (*lip-syncing*): It's certainly either a work of genius or complete insanity. Hard to tell!
JACK (*lip-syncing*): *Waiting for Godot* is categorically the most boring play I've have ever seen, but I have seen it.
CORDELIA (*lip-syncing*): Absolutely revolutionary! People are going to be talking about this for years to come!

JACK (*lip-syncing*): So, am I selling *Godot* to you? (*Laughter.*) But of course all this changed after the première – and soon the play where nothing happens and two characters wait for a third character who never turns up...

ALL (*lip-syncing*): Sorry, spoiler there—

JACK (*lip-syncing*): ...went on to become a classic that still speaks to people across the world today, on a deeply personal level. But why did it provoke such a strong reaction after the première in 1955? How did it break new ground?

JOSIE (*lip-syncing*): Well, conventional theatre... it's all in the plot. And it relies on... characterisation... and, er, setting... to demonstrate space and time. But *Godot* was profoundly different to what had come before. Beckett reduced the concept of theatre to its fundamental elements. Actors – on stage – being watched by people. We could feel time passing in real time, between the beginning and the end of the play. And Beckett made that sense of time on stage, the play's length, a kind of metaphor for life. How do we experience time, from the beginning to the end of the day? From our birth to our death?

(*The sound of the hold music fades in again. They look to the phone.*)

JOSIE: That passed the time.
JACK: It would have passed anyway.
CORDELIA: Yeah, but not as quickly.

(*They wait.*)

JOSIE: Can I have a hug?
JACK: Yeah, of course!

(*They hug.*)

CORDELIA: Can I have a hug?
JOSIE: Yeah, of course!

(*They hug. This continues and builds into a sequence of various 'hugs' to pass the time, building in speed and complexity.*)

CORDELIA: Did you hear about the two legends?
JOSIE: Not now.
CORDELIA: It was just a suggestion.

(*They wait. The hold music continues to play. They look at each other, then the audience, then the phone.*)

CORDELIA: Was it definitely the right number?
JOSIE: I think so.
JACK: Perhaps they're closed on Sundays?
JOSIE: But today isn't Sunday.

CORDELIA: Isn't it?
JOSIE: Is it not Tuesday?
JACK: Or Thursday?
CORDELIA: Or Saturday?
JOSIE: I'm sure they'll answer.
JACK: We just have to wait.

(*They wait. Another radio voiceover plays. They all look up, listening this time.*)

RADIO VOICEOVER (*after four radio pips*):

'So we've heard about the idea there of having, say, an all-female production of *Waiting for Godot*, but that's something Samuel Beckett himself opposed... but now, of course, we're in an era concerned with identity politics like never before... so... Do you think this could be possible now? Putting on a production with an all-female cast?'

'I don't think the Estate would go for it. There's a reason Beckett didn't want an all-female cast – for example, Vladimir has prostate problems, so. But there was a court case in... I think in 2006... in the Netherlands, I think, and the court ruled that Vladimir and Estragon could be played by women *playing men*. But I think the fact of the matter is the Estate wouldn't be happy with an all-female production of *Godot* – but, you know,

I have to say, there are productions going on all over the world of *Godot* – and other Beckett plays – and many of them are, well, less respectful of the stage directions than others!

(*A pause.*)

CORDELIA: I didn't like that.
JACK: Me neither.

(*A pause.*)

JOSIE: We're not the first to have tried—
JACK: To have failed—
JOSIE: To have tried! There was a production at Avignon Festival in 1991.
CORDELIA: When the Beckett Estate claimed that the play would be deformed by an all-female cast?
JACK: Deformed?
CORDELIA: Deformed.
JOSIE: The company won the case!
JACK: But a letter of objection from the Estate had to be read before each show.
CORDELIA: Classic.
JOSIE: How about Paris in 1992?
CORDELIA: That was the company that was refused permission to use female actors after a judge said it was a 'violation of Beckett's moral rights'?

JACK: Violation?

CORDELIA: Violation.

JACK: Classic.

JOSIE: What about Edinburgh in 1998? The Estate assured a company that the play could go ahead with two women playing Vladimir and Estragon…

JACK: But the show got pulled just weeks before its run…

CORDELIA: When the Estate ruled that it could bring ridicule upon the author.

JACK: And assumed that the company were a gay-rights group with a political motive for staging a 'transvestite production'.

CORDELIA: Transvestite?

JACK: Transvestite.

CORDELIA: Classic.

(*They are all downtrodden.*)

JOSIE: What about the Italian twins in 2006?

JACK: Oh yes… that's a good one.

CORDELIA: A real breakthrough.

JACK: Another case of a case.

CORDELIA: A court case. Estates love getting lawyers involved.

JOSIE: The two women stepped in after the male actors pulled out of the production and the company won the case!

JACK: But the performers had to play the roles as men.

JOSIE: Right…

CORDELIA: The women presented like men on stage: low voices, bound chests, facial hair…

JACK: So no one would be able to tell they weren't.

CORDELIA: Classic.

JOSIE: 2019!

CORDELIA: Ohio?

JOSIE: Oberlin College…? They tried… didn't they?

JACK: …and were also faced with legal action from the Estate if they continued their plans to stage the play without a male cast.

JOSIE: And so to surmise…

CORDELIA: To summarise…

JACK: To summarise…

CORDELIA: With the very best intentions…

JACK: The very very best intentions…

JOSIE: We say no…

JACK: No.

JOSIE: No.

CORDELIA: No no no.

JACK: You lose.

JOSIE: We win.

ALL: Classic.

(*They all sit.* JACK *takes a carrot out of their pocket and examines it. They go to take a bite when* CORDELIA *stops them.* CORDELIA *takes a vegetable peeler out of her pocket and peels the carrot. When the carrot is fully peeled she puts the peelings in her pocket and hands it back to* JACK. JACK *goes to take a bite, when* JOSIE *reveals her own carrot, stopping* JACK *in their tracks.* CORDELIA *takes* JOSIE*'s carrot and peels it.* JACK *waits.* CORDELIA *then reveals her own carrot and peels it, whilst* JACK *and* JOSIE *wait. Once all three carrots are peeled, they take a bite and spit out the top end in unison. They continue to crunch throughout the following.*)

CORDELIA: How is it?
JACK: It's a carrot.

(*Pause.*)

JOSIE: We have tried before.
JACK: We have.
CORDELIA: Before today.
JACK: There was an email.
CORDELIA: A message.
JOSIE: A letter.
JACK: A correspondence.
JOSIE: A letter.
CORDELIA: We always knew getting the rights wouldn't be easy. Beckett is notoriously strict with his plays; you can't cut lines, you can't change stage directions.

JOSIE: Naturally, they'll have to consider our application.
JACK: Make decisions.
CORDELIA: Take some calls.
JOSIE: Consult their colleagues.
JACK: Their acquaintances.
JOSIE: Their followers.
JACK: Their next-door neighbours.
CORDELIA: Until now we've only made our own, slightly niche, plays.
JOSIE: A silent clown show about corporate responsibility and a dance piece about depression.
JACK: Not big money-spinners.
CORDELIA: *Waiting for Godot* would be our opportunity to branch out, reach new people, extend our crowd.
JOSIE: It's a classic.

(They notice a hat on the floor and begin a hat-swapping sequence that escalates until it reaches a peak. The sequence is suddenly interrupted by a clip from 'Vogue' by Madonna. They appear to strut forward involuntarily and look baffled until…)

CORDELIA: Where was I? Ah yes, the two legends … you know this, don't you?
JACK: No.
CORDELIA: Shall I tell it to you?
JACK: No.

CORDELIA (*pause*): Two legends... living legends... infamous... prolific...

JACK: Who?

CORDELIA: Two legends... renowned... celebrated... equals to McKellen and Stewart...

JACK: Wait... what?

CORDELIA: How is it – I hope this is not boring you – how is it that even Maggie Smith and Fiona Shaw didn't dare do it?

JACK: What?

CORDELIA: *Waiting for Godot*.

JACK: Right...

CORDELIA: They wanted to but... after the Beckett Estate shut down their 1994 production of *Footfalls* – because the director had cut five lines from the script, allowed Fiona Shaw to move around the stage and decided to change the colour of her dress from grey to red – they thought they'd just do *Happy Days* instead – and Fiona vowed that she'd stay in her hole, 'as Beckett intended'.

JACK: Classic.

JOSIE: It's a classic.

(*Pause. They wait. The hold music fades in.*)

JACK: Hey, this is what they do.

CORDELIA: What who do?

JACK: What they do.

CORDELIA: Who?
JACK: Vladimir and Estragon!
CORDELIA: Didi and Gogo!
JACK: Yes! This is what they do!
CORDELIA: What who do?
JACK: What they do. Didi and Gogo. They wait. (*Pause.*) Just wait. And they talk. They wait and talk.
JOSIE: And they dance.
JACK: Wait and talk and dance.
CORDELIA: And think.
JACK: Wait and talk and dance and think.
JOSIE: For what?
CORDELIA: What?
JOSIE: Wait for what?
CORDELIA: For who?
JACK: For whom.
JOSIE: Wait for whom?
CORDELIA: For Godot.
JOSIE: Not us.
JACK: No, them.
CORDELIA: Yes, them.
JACK: And they meet other people.
JOSIE: They do. Two other people.
JACK: Three.
CORDELIA: Two or three.
JOSIE: But not Godot.
JACK: And the hats…

CORDELIA: And the carrots...
JOSIE: And the boots.
ALL: Of course, the boots. (*Pause.*) And the carrots. (*Longer pause.*) And the hats.
JACK: They say they'll leave.
CORDELIA: But they don't.
JACK: They say they'll leave but they don't leave.
JOSIE: Leave for the night.
ALL: But they do not move.

(*They stay resolutely still, deliberately not moving a muscle. The opening of 'Like Sugar' by Chaka Khan begins to play. They fight the urge to dance as the music builds. When the music finally drops, they dance a sharply choreographed but ridiculous routine.* CORDELIA *and* JOSIE *continue getting increasingly 'sexy' until they are interrupted by* JACK *in a mad frenzy, shouting.*)

JACK: THIS IS WHY YOU CAN'T DO IT. YOU SLUTS. YOU BITCHES. YOU JUST HAVE TO MAKE IT SEXY. YOU BINTS, WHORES, WENCHES. YOU STUPID WOMEN...
CORDELIA: Jack?
JACK: GETTING YOUR TITTIES ALL OVER MY FAVOURITE PLAY...
JOSIE: Jack?
JACK: I'M NOT JACK, I'M SAMUEL BECKETT, YOU BITCH.

(JACK *gradually calms down.*)

JOSIE: Are you OK?
JACK: I think I just wanted to see it from his perspective.
CORDELIA: Whose?
JACK: Samuel Beckett's. I just needed to get into his head for a minute.
JOSIE: So that was an Irish accent?
JACK: …Yeah.

(*A pause.*)

JACK: Maybe it's the testosterone.

(JOSIE *and* CORDELIA *silently agree.*)

JOSIE: Do you think Beckett really thought like that?
CORDELIA: No.
JACK: Maybe.
CORDELIA: I don't know.
PHONE VOICEOVER: You are number – 4,376 – in the call queue.

(*The hold music continues. They are starting to get bored now.*)

JACK: We could just do it.
CORDELIA: What?

JACK: We could just do it.
JOSIE: But we can't.
JACK: But we could…
JOSIE: If we tried…
CORDELIA: But we won't.

(*A pause.*)

JACK: We should.
JOSIE: We could.
CORDELIA: We would… if we had the means.
JACK: But we don't.
JOSIE: But we might…
JACK: If we tried.
JOSIE: We might…
CORDELIA: If we tried.
JACK: But we can't.
CORDELIA: So we don't.
JOSIE: We won't.
CORDELIA: But we could…
JACK: We can't.
JOSIE: We could…
CORDELIA: We can't.
JOSIE: Why not?
JACK: Why try?
JOSIE: Why not?
JACK: Because…
JOSIE: Because what?

CORDELIA: Because we can't.
JOSIE: Who says?
JACK: I say.
JOSIE: You say?
CORDELIA: They say.
JOSIE: Who even are they?
JACK: Enough!

(*A pause.*)

JACK: But we could…
JOSIE: We should…
CORDELIA: We would… if we had the means.
JOSIE: But we can't.
CORDELIA: We can't.
JACK: We can't.

(*Pause.*)

JOSIE: But, we could… if we pretended to be men…
CORDELIA: Looked like men…
JACK: Acted like men…
JOSIE: That could work.

(*They turn away from the audience and apply fake moustaches to their upper lips. 'Boys' by Charlie XCX plays. They dance a comic routine, exploring masculine poses and comically over-sexualised dance moves.*)

CORDELIA: That was good.
JOSIE: Was it?
JACK: I was very convincing.

(JOSIE *and* CORDELIA *agree and congratulate* JACK *until suddenly...*)

JOSIE: I've got it! Ah yes! I've got it. Hear me out. OK. So. We're women, you and me, we're women, so we can't do it, because... we're women. But Jack, they can't say anything about Jack, because Jack, Jack is not a woman. So... Jack's not a woman so... Jack's not a woman. But then again, Jack's also not a man. And they want them to be played by men. So maybe that's just... as bad...?
JACK: Are you done?
JOSIE: ...Yeah.

(*A pause.*)

JACK: I'm going.
JOSIE: We can't.
JACK: Why not?
CORDELIA: We're waiting for *Waiting for Godot*.

(*They wait. The hold music fades in.*)

JOSIE: I'm sure they'll answer...

CORDELIA: They will.
JACK: And if they don't?
JOSIE: They will.
JACK: But if they don't?
CORDELIA: Then maybe they will tomorrow.
JACK: So what do we do till then?
JOSIE: We wait.

(*They wait.*)

JACK: We could do what they do.
JOSIE: What who do?
JACK: Them. The Beckett Estate.
CORDELIA: What do they do?
JACK: They take a stand.
JOSIE: Make a point.
JACK: Take a stand.
CORDELIA: Take the stand.
JOSIE: I'm not with you.
JACK: Take the stand.
JOSIE: I don't get it.
CORDELIA: Take the stand.
JACK: Take the stand.
CORDELIA: Take your time!
JACK: They take people to court.
JOSIE: Oh.
CORDELIA: So we…
JACK: Yes…

JOSIE: Make a case.
JACK: Take a stand.
CORDELIA: Take the stand.

(JACK *picks up the phone. The hold music continues until…*)

JACK: We'll see you in court!

(*They hang up the phone. Courtroom music plays. They create a courtroom. Introduce the Beckett Estate – the* DEFENCE *– the* JUDGE, *the* JURY *– the audience – and themselves – the* PROSECUTION. *The three performers will play all roles in this scene and frequently change role as necessary. The courtroom should be ridiculous, clearly influenced by the drama of televised courtroom programmes.*)

CORDELIA (*as* JUDGE): All rise.

(*They all rise on to their tiptoes and sink back down again.*)

CORDELIA (*as* JUDGE): The court recognises Silent Faces Theatre company – henceforth known as the prosecution – and the Beckett Estate, representing the late Samuel Beckett – henceforth known as the defence. The charges are as follows: The defence has unfairly and unlawfully prohibited, protested and penalised any non-male performers that attempt to perform Samuel

Beckett's most celebrated play, *Waiting for Godot*. The prosecution ask that the rights to perform this play be granted to any company, regardless of their gender. Defence: how do you respond to this charge?

JACK (*as* DEFENCE): Your Honour, with respect to the prosecution, we disagree entirely. We represent a man who offered groundbreaking work to the world of art, and by doing so changed the course of theatrical history for ever. Isn't it therefore reasonable to agree that the artist's wishes in regards to the gender of performers be respected and maintained?

(*Noises of agreement from the defence team.*)

CORDELIA (*as* JUDGE): A very reasonable retort. Prosecution, would you like to respond?
JOSIE (*as* PROSECUTION): We would, your honour.
CORDELIA (*as* JUDGE): Very well…
JOSIE (*as* PROSECUTION): What… now—?
CORDELIA (*as* JUDGE, *cutting over, impatient*): —You have the floor!
JOSIE (*as* PROSECUTION, *uncertain and babbling*): Thank you. Samuel Beckett is a very famous and respected playwright, but this shouldn't stop his work being questioned. The Beckett Estate has no reason to uphold this outdated decision!

CORDELIA (*as* JUDGE, *with disdain*): Very well. Let's proceed. Defence, would you like to call your first witness?

JACK (*as* DEFENCE): We would, your honour. Call to the stand Mr Barrett, a celebrated copyright lawyer.

(*Courtroom music plays.* JACK, *as* COPYRIGHT LAWYER, *takes the stand.* CORDELIA *takes the position of* DEFENCE, JOSIE *as* JUDGE. *The large copy of* Waiting for Godot *descends into view and the witness swears on it like a Bible.*)

JOSIE (*as* JUDGE): Do you promise to tell the truth, the whole truth and nothing but the truth so help you God-ot?

JACK (*as* COPYRIGHT LAWYER): I do.

CORDELIA (*as* DEFENCE): Mr Barrett, could you please tell the jury what it is you do.

JACK (*as* COPYRIGHT LAWYER): I'm a copyright lawyer.

CORDELIA (*as* DEFENCE): And in your professional opinion, who holds the power to decide which companies are allowed to perform *Waiting for Godot*?

JACK (*as* COPYRIGHT LAWYER): Well, since Mr Beckett's death in 1989 – God rest his soul – the ownership of his works has been entrusted to his estate.

CORDELIA (*as* DEFENCE): So, in your professional opinion, it is within the Estate's legal power to refuse the performance rights to anyone?

JACK (*as* COPYRIGHT LAWYER): Yes, it is.

CORDELIA (*as* DEFENCE): And this could be for any artistic reason?

JACK (*as* COPYRIGHT LAWYER): That is correct.

CORDELIA (*as* DEFENCE): Even if that artistic reason might seem to conflict with discrimination laws?

JACK (*as* COPYRIGHT LAWYER): I would say yes. Any artistic reason would be a valid ground for refusal.

CORDELIA (*as* DEFENCE): Thank you, Mr Barrett. The defence rests, your honour.

JOSIE (*as* JUDGE, *suddenly*): Prosecution, would you like to cross-examine the witness?

(JOSIE *has confused herself and fumbles into playing the* PROSECUTION.)

JOSIE (*as* PROSECUTION, *baffled and unprepared*): Err… we would, your honour. Mr Barrett, it says here that you have been a copyright lawyer for forty-four years; is that correct?

JACK (*as* COPYRIGHT LAWYER): Yes, that's correct.

JOSIE (*as* PROSECUTION): So you're an expert – you must have dealt with a lot of copyright cases?

JACK (*as* COPYRIGHT LAWYER): Well, indeed, yes, naturally.

JOSIE (*as* PROSECUTION): And, as an expert, do you believe that only men should perform *Waiting for Godot?*
JACK (*as* COPYRIGHT LAWYER, *scoffing*): Well, it's not about what I believe.
JOSIE (*as* PROSECUTION): No… Of course not… I… (*Flicks through her documents.*)

(*Awkward pause.*)

CORDELIA (*as* JUDGE): Prosecution, have you any further questions prepared? No? In that case I can only see fit to terminate this cross-examination. Mr Barrett, you may step down. Defence, would you like to call a second witness?

(JACK *takes the place of the* DEFENCE.)

JACK (*as* DEFENCE): Thank you, your honour. Call to the stand Cordelia Stevenson, of Silent Faces Theatre company.

(*Shocked noises and mutterings.* CORDELIA *becomes herself as* JOSIE *takes the place of* JUDGE. *Courtroom music plays.* CORDELIA *takes the stand.*)

JOSIE (*as* JUDGE): Do you swear to tell the truth, the whole truth and nothing but the truth so help you God-ot?

CORDELIA: I do

JACK (*as* DEFENCE): Your name and occupation, please.

CORDELIA: Cordelia Stevenson, theatre-maker... and part-time receptionist.

(*In the following exchange* JACK *barely allows* CORDELIA *time to answer, frequently cutting over her answers.*)

JACK (*as* DEFENCE): How would you describe yourself in relation to Beckett's work?

CORDELIA: Well, I'm a big fan of his work. I studied a lot of his plays at university and he's been a huge influence on—

JACK (*as* DEFENCE): And how familiar are you with his collection of plays?

CORDELIA: I would say I'm quite familiar... probably a lot more familiar than most. I'm a bit of a nerd—

JACK (*as* DEFENCE): List for me, if you will, the most popular of Samuel Beckett's plays?

CORDELIA: Well, *Waiting for Godot*, of course, *Happy Days*, *Not I*, *Rough for Theatre*, *Act Without Words I* and *II*, *Endgame*—

JACK (*as* DEFENCE): And could you please tell the jury, who may not be as familiar with Beckett's work, who the principal character of *Happy Days* is?

CORDELIA: That would be Winnie.

JACK (*as* DEFENCE): And could you describe the intended gender of Winnie?

CORDELIA: Intended…? (*Pause.*) She's female.

JACK (*as* DEFENCE): So it is fair to say that among Beckett's works there are parts written for women?

CORDELIA: Well, yes… but they're not exactly what you would call—

JACK (*as* DEFENCE): Large roles, in fact. Is it or is it not true that *Happy Days* is almost entirely a female monologue?

CORDELIA: Yes, but that's not really the point that we're getting—

JACK (*as* DEFENCE): And is it not also true that *Not I*, *Footfalls*, *Rockabye*, *Play* – all works by Samuel Beckett– have large roles intended for female performers?

CORDELIA: That's true, but if you look at the rest of Beckett's works, there's quite a lot of—

JACK (*as* DEFENCE): So it is possible for a company of female performers who wanted to perform a Beckett play to find a multitude of characters that are intended for them?

CORDELIA: Well, I wouldn't… exactly say that—

JACK (*as* DEFENCE): See, your honour. As Miss Stevenson has just admitted, there are a number of Beckett's plays that have wonderful, large, respected roles for women. We would argue that the company are deliberately finding fault with the Estate and would be better off spending their time working on plays that were written for them, rather than creating all this fuss around a play that just doesn't fit their casting. No further questions, your honour.

JOSIE (*as* JUDGE): Thank you. That seems a very fair argument. If there are no further questions—

CORDELIA (*as* JUDGE, *frustrated*): Would you like to cross-examine the witness?

CORDELIA (*as* PROSECUTION): We would, your honour. Miss Stevenson, why would you rather perform *Waiting for Godot* over a Beckett text intended for female performers?

CORDELIA (*as herself*): Thanks for asking. Well … because *Waiting for Godot* is about a shared human experience. Yes, Beckett wrote roles for women, but look at them! *Happy Days*, 1961. Winnie.

(CORDELIA *reads a section of the character description of Winnie from* Happy Days. *As she speaks, the lights fade to darkness and a single focused light slowly appears around her mouth.*)

Blonde, bare, bodice, bosom, buried. Buried up to her waist. Buried up to her neck. Submerged, sinking. Trapped, but still smiling. Go on, give us a smile – it could be worse – you're prettier when you smile. Prattle, chatter, blether, blather. Nothing of consequence, no respect, spared that, nothing of anything. What. No. Who. She.

Play, 1963. Man. Wife. Mistress. Wife. Mistress. Defined only in relation to Man. Man, singular, solo, standing. Wife. Mistress. Belonging to. Objects for.

You degrade us, depicting us as less than the sum of our parts. Yes, less. Tiny little things, godforsaken things. Part woman – no, part girl – and part object. Reduced to head, torso, mouth; taken apart. No. Not me. Not I. A few steps then stop, a few more, then stop. Progress, protest, prohibited. In control, under control, don't question this. Fifty years, fifty years and still this.

(*The lights snap back to full.*)

No further questions, your honour.
JOSIE (*as* JUDGE): Thank you, Miss Stevenson. You may step down. Defence, would you like to call your third witness?
JACK (*as* DEFENCE): Thank you, your honour. Two witnesses, in fact. A duo, if you will. Not one, but two medical professionals.

(JOSIE *and* JACK *become* DR WIMPLE *and* DR WOMPLE.)

CORDELIA (*as* DEFENCE): Not one! But two! Medical professionals!

(*Music plays and the* DOCTORS *enter, waving to the audience.*)

JOSIE (*as* DR WIMPLE): I am Dr Wimple.
JACK (*as* DR WOMPLE): And I am Dr Womple.
BOTH: And we are very serious medical professionals.

(*The following is a description of the prostate in the style of a vintage informational film. Music plays.*)

JOSIE (*as* DR WIMPLE): You don't all have one, but you all know someone who does.
JACK (*as* DR WOMPLE): That's got you thinking, hasn't it? Right now, there's almost certainly one in this room. Can you feel that? Can you feel its presence? That's right, I'm talking about…

(*A card is flipped over, revealing an anatomical image of a penis, with the prostate labelled.*)

BOTH: The prostate.

(*They point at the prostate with a telescopic pointer, followed by a 'ding' sound. This ding sound and the telescopic pointer are used frequently throughout the following to highlight information.*)

JACK (*as* DR WOMPLE): There he is. Look, he's waving!

JOSIE (*as* DR WIMPLE): But what *is* the prostate?

JACK (*as* DR WOMPLE): Approximately the size of a walnut… (*pulls a walnut out of their pocket and shells it*) …the prostate, located between the bladder and the penis, is a gland which secretes fluid that nourishes and protects sperm. Nice work, prostate! (*They eat the walnut.*)

JOSIE (*as* DR WIMPLE): Practically every man over the age of fifty experiences benign prostatic hypertrophy, or… BPH.

JACK (*as* DR WOMPLE): Meaning…

JOSIE (*as* DR WIMPLE): Benign.

JACK (*as* DR WOMPLE): Not harmful.

JOSIE (*as* DR WIMPLE): Prostatic.

JACK (*as* DR WOMPLE): Of the prostate.

JOSIE (*as* DR WIMPLE): Hypertrophy.

JACK (*as* DR WOMPLE): Enlargement.

JOSIE (*as* DR WIMPLE): In short? The prostate increases in size, pressing against the bladder.

JACK (*as* DR WOMPLE): Steady on there, pal! (*They playfully swat the prostate with the pointer.*)

JOSIE (*as* DR WIMPLE): Possible symptoms of BPH include: A sudden urge to urinate. Difficulty starting to urinate. Dribbling urine after you finish urinating. And needing to urinate more often, especially at night. Now, none of this will kill you, fellas, but it's certainly a real pain in the proverbial.

(*The music ends and the* DOCTORS *exit.* CORDELIA *has become the* DEFENCE.)

CORDELIA (*as* DEFENCE): Thank you Dr Wimple. Thank you Dr Womple. Well, that was extraordinarily informative. I will invite the jury to reflect on this evidence in a moment, but first—

(JOSIE *and* JACK *re-enter.*)

JOSIE (*as* PROSECUTION): —What was that?!

(JACK *quickly assumes the position of* JUDGE.)

JACK (*as* JUDGE): Order in court! Does the prosecution have something to say?
JOSIE (*as* PROSECUTION): Yes, your honour. We've come here to take this case seriously, not have fake doctors provide irrelevant evidence—
CORDELIA (*as* DEFENCE): Doctors Wimple and Womple are very serious medical professionals!—
JOSIE (*as* PROSECUTION): Your honour! The prosecution would like to call a real witness.
JACK (*as* JUDGE): Very well, proceed.
JOSIE (*as* PROSECUTION): Call to the stand Jack Wakely.

(*Courtroom music plays and* JACK *takes the stand.* CORDELIA *takes the position of* JUDGE.)

CORDELIA (*as* JUDGE): Do you promise to tell the truth, the whole truth and nothing but the truth, so help you God-ot?

JACK: I do.

JOSIE (*as* PROSECUTION): Jack, how would you describe a man?

JACK: Um... which man?

JOSIE (*as* PROSECUTION): Any man.

JACK: Well, I guess... Just... They're a man – what else can I say?

JOSIE (*as* PROSECUTION): And what is your gender?

JACK: I'm non-binary.

JOSIE (*as* PROSECUTION): And what does being non-binary mean to you?

JACK: Well... what does being female mean to you? I don't think it's actually possible to fully articulate to someone else the experience of your own gender.

JOSIE: Fair point.

CORDELIA (*as* JUDGE, *grumbling and chiming in*): Just answer the question...

JACK: Very, very simply... I'm not male or female; my gender's outside of that binary.

JOSIE (*as* PROSECUTION): And what is your favourite Beckett play?

JACK: *Waiting for Godot*, obviously.

JOSIE (*as* PROSECUTION): But you aren't allowed to perform *Waiting for Godot*?

JACK: No, because I'm not a man.

JOSIE (*as* PROSECUTION): But you are not a woman.

JACK: No.

JOSIE (*as* PROSECUTION): Would you please list, for the jury, the plays or characters that Beckett wrote for non-binary people?

JACK: There aren't any.

JOSIE (*as* PROSECUTION): None at all?

JACK: Not specifically, no.

JOSIE (*as* PROSECUTION): Would you list, for the jury, *any* classic plays with characters specifically written for non-binary people?

JACK: There aren't any.

JOSIE (*as* PROSECUTION): Thank you, Jack. Your honour, in response to the defence's case that we should simply perform the plays that are written for us, we have to point out that there are practically no roles written for people who aren't male *or* female. In fact, *Waiting for Godot* is surely one of the few classic plays where the gender of the characters has absolutely no bearing on the audience's understanding of the piece—

CORDELIA (*as* DEFENCE, *cutting in*): The defence would like to cross-examine the witness!

(*Courtroom music plays.*)

CORDELIA (*as* DEFENCE): Jack Wakely, you say that you identify as non-binary.

JACK: No, no, I said I *am* non-binary.

CORDELIA (*as* DEFENCE): And that means you're neither male nor female?

JACK: I mean, that's an incredibly over-simplified way of looking at it—

CORDELIA (*as* DEFENCE): But for argument's sake, would you say you lean more to the male or the female?

JACK: I'm sorry?

CORDELIA (*as* DEFENCE): For convenience, say, would you lean more towards male or female?

JACK: Neither.

CORDELIA (*as* DEFENCE): But if you had to decide?

JACK: I have decided.

CORDELIA (*as* DEFENCE): If you had to play a male or female role, which would you prefer?

JACK: I'd prefer to play a role that was made for me.

CORDELIA (*as* DEFENCE): But – you can see what I'm getting at here – this gender... thing... it's a fairly recent phenomenon. Can you not appreciate that it might take some time for the world to catch up?

JACK: Oh, of course! We can't be naïve enough to think that things will change instantaneously.

Because, after all, we're a new invention. Haven't you heard? An entire group of people who literally sprang into existence overnight.

CORDELIA: My point exactly.

JACK: I mean, unless you count the fact that there are references to a third gender found throughout the texts of three ancient religions: Hinduism, Buddhism and Jainism. Never mind the ancient Mesopotamian writings from the second millennium BCE, which also describe people that were neither male nor female. Oh, and how about the ancient Egyptian pottery shards that depict men, women and another gender, 'sekhet'? Or the Native American two-spirit people of North America, revered as healers and visionaries until, of course, Europeans invaded, bringing their Colonialist ideas of homophobia and transphobia with them. Or the Māhū of Hawaii, respected as teachers, diviners, caretakers and then, oh, look at that, Europeans invaded again. And then there's Aristophanes' creation myth, or the six genders of old Israel, or ancient Rome's Galli, or the Public Universal Friend. But you're right, apart from all that, we're a real modern phenomenon.

(A pause.)

CORDELIA (*as* DEFENCE): No further questions.

JOSIE (*as* JUDGE): Do you have any further evidence to present?

CORDELIA (*as* DEFENCE): Yes, your honour. If it pleases the court, I will present Exhibit P. An extract from Act One of *Waiting For Godot* depicting... Vladimir's prostate problem.

JOSIE: Objection! At no point in the text does it explicitly say that Vladimir has a prostate!

CORDELIA (*as* DEFENCE): It implies it! There may not be an explicit reference to the—

JOSIE: It implies that Vladimir *might* have a nondescript physical problem, and that he often goes offstage, presumably to wee, but it doesn't say anything about a prostate! Plus, everybody wees!

JACK (*as* DEFENCE): Objection! The prosecution is reducing Samuel Beckett's great work to trivialities. The play is about much more pressing issues than urinating and thumb-twiddling.

CORDELIA (*as* JUDGE): Sustained. Prosecution, can you please present a more solid case than the universal need to urinate?

JOSIE (*as* PROSECUTION): But it is about those things, the things that unite us – regardless of gender!

(*Noises of agreement from the* JUDGE.)

JACK (*as* DEFENCE): Objection! You're reducing the play to a conversation about that, about gender, and it is so much more than that. This is a play about humanity.

JOSIE (*as* PROSECUTION): And we are all human!

JACK (*as* DEFENCE): Objection!

CORDELIA (*as* JUDGE, *quietly*): Sustained.

JACK (*as* DEFENCE): It's unreasonable to ask people to ignore the gender of the performers. It destroys the artistic integrity of the work.

JOSIE (*as* PROSECUTION): Objection!

CORDELIA (*as* JUDGE): Overruled!

JOSIE (*as* PROSECUTION, *ignoring* JUDGE): It's more unreasonable to demand that only men can represent humanity!

JACK (*as* DEFENCE): Objection!

CORDELIA (*as* JUDGE, *quietly*): Sustained.

JACK (*as* DEFENCE): We can't be held responsible for the common opinion of our audience or the public.

JOSIE (*as* PROSECUTION): Can we not have an influence over what is put on our stages?

JACK (*as* DEFENCE): Our priority is to maintain Samuel Beckett's wishes, not to change the world.

JOSIE (*as* PROSECUTION): We've established that Beckett changed the way we view theatre; why can't this be another opportunity for change?

JACK (*as* DEFENCE): Objection!

JOSIE (*as* PROSECUTION): Objection!
CORDELIA (*as* JUDGE): **OBJECTION!**
JOSIE (*as* PROSECUTION): The prosecution would like to re-call a witness!
CORDELIA (*as* JUDGE): What? You can't do that!
JOSIE (*as* PROSECUTION): Overruled! Re-call to the stand Mr Barrett!

(*Courtroom music plays as* JOSIE *becomes Mr Barrett, the* COPYRIGHT LAWYER. *The copy of* Waiting for Godot *comes down and then goes back up very quickly. Mr Barrett is a bit more ridiculous than last time.*)

CORDELIA (*as* PROSECUTION): Mr Barrett, who's your favourite female artist?
JOSIE (*as* COPYRIGHT LAWYER): I'm sorry?
CORDELIA (*as* PROSECUTION): Your favourite female recording artist?
JOSIE (*as* COPYRIGHT LAWYER): What's this got to do with anything?
CORDELIA (*as* PROSECUTION): Just answer the question.
JOSIE (*as* COPYRIGHT LAWYER): Oh, well, um, put me on the spot… Favourite female recording artist… I'm going to have to say… Madonna… oh no, Whitney… Ooo, Celine Dion… No no no, Madonna.
CORDELIA (*as* PROSECUTION): Is that your final answer?

JOSIE (*as* COPYRIGHT LAWYER): Yes. Madonna. Final answer.
CORDELIA (*as* PROSECUTION): And do you have a favourite Madonna song?
JOSIE (*as* COPYRIGHT LAWYER): 'Like a Prayer'. No question. Final answer.
CORDELIA (*as* PROSECUTION): And why is that, Mr Barrett?
JOSIE (*as* COPYRIGHT LAWYER): Well, it's a classic.
CORDELIA (*as* PROSECUTION): A classic?
JOSIE (*as* COPYRIGHT LAWYER): Yes, it takes me back to my youth. Everything was changing back then, and we embraced it, but these days everyone just seems so angry.

(*There is a courtroom sting and the cast swap positions. Mr Barrett is more ridiculous.*)

JACK (*as* PROSECUTION): I see, so you would argue that Madonna was an influential artist?
CORDELIA (*as* COPYRIGHT LAWYER): Oh yes, absolutely. She was a real rebel!
JACK (*as* PROSECUTION): Would you mind explaining that statement?
CORDELIA (*as* COPYRIGHT LAWYER): Well, she did a lot that just hadn't been done before. Painted women in a different light. And it wasn't just

women, either. She was a great advocate for gay rights and racial equality.

JACK (*as* PROSECUTION): So you would agree that with the emergence of artists like Madonna, the world – yourself included – started to see women, people of colour, the LGBTQ+ community, all kinds of different people, as more equal citizens?

CORDELIA (*as* COPYRIGHT LAWYER): Well, I guess so, yes.

(Courtroom sting and the cast swap positions. Mr Barrett is even more ridiculous.)

JOSIE (*as* PROSECUTION): Mr Barrett, do you happen to know the year that Madonna released her 'Like a Prayer' album?

CORDELIA (*as* DEFENCE): Objection! The prosecution is side-tracking the witness!

JACK (*as* JUDGE): What's the relevance of this question?

JOSIE (*as* PROSECUTION): It is relevant – just give me a moment.

JACK (*as* JUDGE): Very well, proceed.

JOSIE (*as* PROSECUTION): Mr Barrett...

(Courtroom sting and the cast swap positions.)

CORDELIA (*as* PROSECUTION): When did Madonna release 'Like a Prayer'?

JACK (*as* COPYRIGHT LAWYER): Oh, I have no idea, I'm afraid…

CORDELIA (*as* PROSECUTION): It was 1989, over thirty years ago.

JACK (*as* COPYRIGHT LAWYER): Oh really? That long ago?

CORDELIA (*as* PROSECUTION): With the Judge's permission we would like to play a piece of musical evidence that I think will help us highlight our argument.

JOSIE (*as* JUDGE): Permission granted.

CORDELIA (*as* PROSECUTION): The prosecution calls forward **EXHIBIT X**.

(A megamix begins: each era of history is accompanied by a musical track from that year. 'End of Time' by Beyoncé plays.)

JOSIE: As a demonstration of how far we've come…

CORDELIA: The progress we have made…

JACK: The changes we have seen…

JOSIE: We present to you…

ALL: A timeline of feminist progress since 1989.

CORDELIA: You first.

JACK: No, after you.

JOSIE: I insist.

(*'Like a Prayer' by Madonna plays.*)

JACK: 1989: the world mourns the death of the late, great Samuel Beckett.

(*'Groove Is in the Heart' by Deee-Lite plays.*)

JOSIE: 1991: Anita Hill makes history after testifying that Supreme Court nominee Clarence Thomas had sexually harassed her at work.

(*'Dreams' by Gabrielle plays.*)

CORDELIA: 1994: thirty-two women are ordained as the first female priests in the Church of England.

(*'What You Waiting For?' by Gwen Stefani plays.*)

JACK: 2004: the Gender Recognition Act is amended to also apply to transgender people.

(*'Put Your Records On' by Corinne Bailey Rae plays.*)

JOSIE: 2006: Tarana Burke begins using the phrase 'Me Too' on Myspace, starting a movement to empower women of colour to share their experiences of sexual abuse.

(*'Mercy' by Duffy plays.*)

CORDELIA: 2008: Rebecca Lenkiewicz becomes the first living female playwright to have a play performed on the main stage of the National Theatre.

(*'Pound the Alarm' by Nicki Minaj plays.*)

JOSIE: 2012: women participate in every sport at the Olympics for the first time.

(*'Work Bitch' by Britney Spears plays.*)

CORDELIA: 2013: the US military removes a ban against women serving in combat positions.

(*'Bad Blood' by Taylor Swift plays.*)

JACK: 2015: Harvey Weinstein is questioned by police after Ambra Gutierrez comes forward with allegations of sexual assault.

(*'Work' by Rihanna ft. Drake plays.*)

CORDELIA: 2016: Hillary Clinton becomes the first woman to receive a presidential nomination for a major political party.

(*'New Rules' by Dua Lipa plays.*)

CORDELIA: 2017: the Weinstein case blows up.
JACK: 'Hashtag Me Too' is reprised as a way for people to share their experiences of sexual abuse.
JOSIE: Survivors everywhere come forward. And not just in Hollywood...
JOSIE: But in theatre...
JACK: Music...
CORDELIA: Politics...
JACK: Religion...
JOSIE: Sport...
CORDELIA: Business...

(*'Bad Guy' by Billie Eilish plays.*)

CORDELIA: 2019...
JACK: After a campaign by Gina Martin, upskirting is made illegal in the UK.
JOSIE: And our galaxy sees its first all-female space walk.

(*'Rain on Me' by Lady Gaga and Ariana Grande plays.*)

JACK: 2020...
JOSIE: And Harvey Weinstein is sentenced to twenty-three years in prison.

(*They dance until* JACK *finds their way back to becoming the* DEFENCE.)

JACK (*as* DEFENCE): Objection!
CORDELIA (*as* JUDGE): On what grounds?
JACK (*as* DEFENCE): We have a lunch at the golf club at noon…
JOSIE (*as* PROSECUTION): Mr Barrett, would you agree that towards the end of the 1980s society was beginning to witness a break down in the barriers between men and women?
CORDELIA (*as* COPYRIGHT LAWYER): Yes. I think that's fair to say.
JOSIE (*as* PROSECUTION): And since that time we have also seen a much-needed re-evaluation of reductive gender binaries?
JACK (*as* DEFENCE): Objection, your honour! The prosecution is confusing the witness with baffling terminology.
CORDELIA (*as* COPYRIGHT LAWYER): I'm not baffled in any way…
JOSIE (*as* PROSECUTION): Do you agree that since the 80s we have come to realise that historically gender has been quite restrictive?
CORDELIA (*as* COPYRIGHT LAWYER): Oh yes.
JOSIE (*as* PROSECUTION): So you would count yourself as one of the many people that supports this change?

CORDELIA (*as* COPYRIGHT LAWYER): Yes.

JOSIE (*as* PROSECUTION): So is it possible to believe that, had he been around to witness the changing world since Madonna's 'Like a Prayer', even Samuel Beckett might have changed his views on women, or at least on the way that women are perceived?

CORDELIA (*as* COPYRIGHT LAWYER): I suppose he might…

JOSIE (*as* PROSECUTION): And had he lived to see the world as it is today, it might have been easier for Beckett to imagine a non-male version of *Waiting for Godot*?

CORDELIA (*as* COPYRIGHT LAWYER): Well, maybe there is an argument for that…

JOSIE (*as* PROSECUTION): But he didn't live past the 1980s, did he?

CORDELIA (*as* COPYRIGHT LAWYER): No.

JOSIE (*as* PROSECUTION): No, he died in 1989.

CORDELIA (*as* COPYRIGHT LAWYER): Yes.

JOSIE (*as* PROSECUTION): So we can't know for sure that he would maintain his original position.

CORDELIA (*as* COPYRIGHT LAWYER): Quite right.

JOSIE (*as* PROSECUTION): And didn't you yourself say it was of the utmost importance to maintain Beckett's views?

CORDELIA (*as* COPYRIGHT LAWYER): Yes, that's right.

JOSIE (*as* PROSECUTION): And yet you can't be certain of what those views might be now, in a time where we have witnessed change after change after change in the equality movement, not only in courts of law, but also via the immovable power of Madonna's music?

(*A pause.*)

JOSIE (*as* PROSECUTION): Mr Barrett, when was the last time that Samuel Beckett actively put a stop to a female production of *Waiting for Godot*?

CORDELIA (*as* COPYRIGHT LAWYER): I... I believe it was in 1988.

JOSIE (*as* COPYRIGHT LAWYER): And again, Mr Barrett, if you please, when did Madonna release 'Like a Prayer'?

CORDELIA (*as* COPYRIGHT LAWYER, *after a deep breath*): 1989.

JOSIE: You see, it is all well and good for the Beckett Estate to want to uphold Samuel Beckett's views, but it has now been over three decades since his death, and it is not possible to argue that Beckett would maintain his decision now.

The reason for restricting these roles might be to 'maintain artistic integrity', Your Honour, but the reality is that it further perpetuates the idea that women and non-binary people don't have the same wonderful, infuriating, painful, confounding, confusing, exciting, terrifying experience of human existence as men. It preserves the idea that there is a fundamental worth in man that cannot be found in others. And it further prolongs the idea that there is an inherent binary in humankind that separates us.

Waiting for Godot is an everyman story. It's a play about humanity, about existence. About not knowing what is coming, and carrying the fuck on anyway. To argue that only men are able to play these parts because otherwise the story would be unbelievable is to say that only men know what it is like to truly exist. That only men know what it is to live and breathe and question and die.

(*'Like a Prayer' begins to play.*)

Well, if the rest of us can see ourselves in man – which we are forced to do all the time – then men can see themselves in everybody else, and, your honour, you should impose that the Beckett Estate should henceforth be prohibited from restricting actors the rights to perform Samuel Beckett's plays based solely on their gender.

(*The music drops into the first chorus and all of them dance. As the music slows we see the* COPYRIGHT LAWYER *ripping up his papers and shaking the hands of the* PROSECUTION. *They are handed a trophy and a baby's head to kiss. A banner that reads 'Silent Faces Win Feminism' unfurls above them. The song's chorus returns and they dance. The chorus returns again and they remove their suits to reveal sparkly outfits. The music slowly fades and we begin to hear hold music again. The banner falls down. The courtroom has entirely faded. They are left with the phone off the hook and the sound of the hold music playing on and on.*)

JOSIE: Nothing to be done.
CORDELIA: Nothing to be done.
JACK: Enough!

(*A pause.*)

CORDELIA: What'll we do?
JACK: What can we do?
JOSIE: Something different.
JACK: Than before?
CORDELIA: Something new.
JOSIE: Something better.
CORDELIA: Something new.

(*A pause.*)

JOSIE: This is the problem. We're trying to do their play…

JACK: Play their game.

CORDELIA: There's man, blaming on his shoes the failings of his feet.

JOSIE: There's woman, blaming on her feet the failings of her shoes... Their game wasn't built for us. We need to rewrite the game...

CORDELIA: Not play by their rules.

JACK: Rewrite the rules...

CORDELIA: Change the game.

(*Pause.*)

JOSIE: Why are you talking like that?

CORDELIA: Like what?

JOSIE: Like that.

JACK: Like what?

JOSIE: You know.

JACK: Like what?

JOSIE: Like that.

CORDELIA: Like this?

JOSIE: Yes. Like that.

CORDELIA: I'm not.

JOSIE: You're not?

JACK: I'm not. Why are you talking like that?

JOSIE: Like what?

CORDELIA: Like that.

JOSIE: I'm not.

JACK: Neither am I.

CORDELIA: Neither am I.
JACK: We... are... not...
JOSIE: Stop.
CORDELIA: We're not getting anywhere.
JACK: Not going anywhere.
JOSIE: Not getting anywhere.
JACK: Not going anywhere.
CORDELIA: Stop!
JOSIE: We've stopped.

(*A pause.*)

CORDELIA: Well, let's start moving.
JOSIE: Let's start moving.

(*'Hammer' by Tune-Yards plays and the sound of a tree falling is heard. They dance and tear down the tree until it is uprooted.*)

JACK: I'm going.

(JACK *leaves and the others slowly follow. The stage is empty. The phone rings.*)

CURTAIN

ACKNOWLEDGEMENTS

Thank you to the wonderful people at The Pleasance, without whom this show would not have been possible. Special thanks to Ryan Ford, Marec Joyce, Eppie Conrad, Kathleen Price, Emily Holland, Anthony Alderson, Nic Connaughton, Ellie Simpson and Jonny Patton.

We are also hugely grateful to the teams at Camden People's Theatre and New Diorama who have supported us in our work and company progression to date.

A special thank you to our brilliant colleagues, designers and friends. To our magnificent production manager Stella Kailides, our tremendous director Laura Killeen, the brilliant Rachel Gammon and Fran Gibson for their costume and set design, to our unflappable lighting designer Jo Palmer and the extraordinarily patient and talented Ellie Isherwood, our sound designer. Special thanks to Cara Withers for heroically jumping into Cordelia's boots after the broken foot disaster of May 2021. Thanks also to Lauren Gibson, Sarah Kelly and Jenny Swingler, who were invaluable in the room so early in the process.

Thank you to our generous funders, Arts Council England, Garfield Weston, The Cockayne Foundation and The Pleasance, and to all those who graciously donated to our crowdfunder for Edinburgh Festival Fringe 2022.

Thanks also to Bart Gwynn, Ros Watt, Grace Dickson, Alex Stringer, Carmel Macaree, Josie Shipp, Mikkaila Mckeever-Willis, Emma Croad, all the Degenerate Foxes, Lesley, Neil and James Stevenson, Lewis, Bev, Nige and Jack Bray, John and Marion Evans and Lu, Sandy, Sam and George Underwood.

Thank you to all of the artists and companies who have fiercely and passionately fought their case to perform *Waiting for Godot* with a non-male cast since 1953, who dared to challenge the Estate where we did not.

Finally, thank you to Samuel Beckett, whose work we love and whose genius and style will always have an imprint on Silent Faces' present, past and future work.

ABOUT SILENT FACES

Silent Faces have been making seriously silly theatre since 2015. Combining their unique style of physical theatre, clowning, mime and new writing, they create high-concept devised theatre that tackles big issues. They are a female and non-binary led integrated company of disabled and non-disabled artists, whose work has been performed at The Pleasance London, Edinburgh Fringe, Camden People's Theatre, Latitude Festival, Wilderness Festival, Brighton Fringe and as part of Incoming Festival at HOME Manchester and New Diorama. Previous productions to date include the 'comic and compelling' (*The Stage*) *Follow Suit* and the 'deceptively playful' (*New York Times*) *A Clown Show About Rain*.

Their work has been supported by Arts Council England, The Cockayne Foundation, Garfield Weston, The Pleasance, Camden People's Theatre, New Diorama and Disability Arts Online and has received critical acclaim from *The Guardian*, *The Stage*, *The Scotsman*, *Exeunt* and *The Spectator*.

www.silentfaces.uk

CORDELIA

Cordelia Stevenson (she/her) is Co-Artistic Director of Silent Faces and is a theatre-maker, director, facilitator, actor, clown and producer. As a director and facilitator, she has worked with organisations including the National Theatre, Splendid Productions, Goldsmiths College, Poplar Union and Jackson's Lane. Cordelia seeks to promote accessibility within her work and is passionate about clowning as a radical and empowering form for those who have historically been excluded from male-centric clown and actor training.

JACK

Jack Wakely (they/them) is a theatre-maker, actor, director, producer, writer and Co-Artistic Director of Silent Faces. They are an advocate for increasing accessibility to the arts, and recognising and elevating gender diversity, invisible disabilities and neurodiversity within them. Jack is a founding member of Degenerate Fox (AKA the London Neo-Futurists), performing regularly in *The Dirty Thirty*, a fortnightly outing of thirty original plays performed in one hour.

JOSIE

Josie Underwood (she/her) is Co-Artistic Director and Managing Director of Silent Faces. She is a director, movement director, actor and producer. She is passionate about making engaging theatre that encourages debate and raises awareness of urgent societal issues, in both content and practice. Josie also works with Freelancers Make Theatre Work, an organisation advocating for the 200,000+ freelance workers who make up seventy per cent of the UK theatre workforce.